CW01095214

Other titles by Sonam Kaur:

*Coffee, a Notebook and Self Love*

*From Dusk Till Dawn*

# Beholden

This book is wholeheartedly dedicated to my mum, Daljit.
Me, my family and friends lost my mum in June 2021 to pancreatic cancer.
She passed away peacefully, surrounded by her family 2 days before her 57th birthday.

Her cancer journey was so difficult for her, for all of us but it also made me appreciate our relationship so much and hold my loved ones so dearly.

She was always so supportive of my writing, sometimes she didn't understand it, but she was always there in my corner.

I reminisce and I am so thankful that you are my mum.

I miss you every second of the day.

This one is for you.

# <u>Mourning</u>

*noun [ U ]*

*great sadness felt because someone has died:*

*TW: Death, Grief, Suicidal Thoughts.*

Mum,
But you are more than that,
Nanni,
Daughter,
Sister
Wife,
Auntie,
Friend,
You are all of that,
So many roles you play,
In people's lives,
I am so glad they got,
To experience some of your life,
Because,
Mum you are truly one of a kind,
I have never seen someone,
Who loves as much as you do,
Our family,
Is so strong and it's all because of you,
You've been though your fair share of shit,
And if I could make a wish,
It's that you wouldn't have gone through,
Any of this,
You we're scared to leave us,
And we're scared too,
But,
I know grandad,
Is waiting for you,
His arms are open,
And I know he will,
Take care of you.
You may be gone,
You will never really be gone,
You are half of me,
Half of us,
Nobody could ever,
Replace you,
You are forever,
Our mum.

You are someone I worship,
Who's feet I would fall at,
In my darkest nights,
And my brightest days,
I learn from you,
Then follow what you have taught,
Then,
Integrate them into my life,
I look to you,
For guidance,
For an answer,
To this sadness,
To my prayers.

How do I go on,
When there is a dark hole,
Consuming my soul,
I look okay,
I should be okay,
Right?
I can go to a celebration,
I should be able to go,
To anything,
I should be able to,
Show up.

Nobody can prepare you,
For how dark this life can be,
How one day,
It all makes sense,
And the next,
You don't have a clue,
Nobody knows,
How it feels to be you,
The challenges that you face,
How it all effects you,
Don't listen to them,
When they tell you,
How you should feel,
Or hit you with the,
Response that starts with,
At least..
At least nothing,
Don't let them tell you,
How to feel.

Don't let them tell you how to feel.

Make it make sense to me,
Make something,
Make sense,
I'd ask for anything,
Right now,
Just something,
That doesn't make me,
Question this space,
Question this time,
This place,
You should be here.

They say you are supposed to float,
When you are drowning,
But what about,
When you aren't floating,
Nor drowning.

What I would do,
To be stood,
Out in this rain,
With you.

They keep placing weights,
On my back,
Stacks and stacks,
They want me,
To break down,
They want it to,
Crack.

-   *Which straw broke the camel's back?*

There is something,
About,
That frenemy,
Called death,
It comes around,
And rips your,
Whole existence,
To shreds.

There you are,
In the starring role,
Or even,
If it's just a feature,
I get to see you,
Hear your voice,
It's like you never left,
It's so good,
To have you,
To hold you,
I miss you.

Just know,
I am missing you,
Ever,
So silently.

I know I am not alone,
In my grief,
But now,
I am a lonely soul,
Searching,
For relief.

Life without you,
Like the,
Winter sky,
Grey,
Blue.

I long to see you,
See how well,
You are doing,
Without me,
See that,
All my,
Well wishes,
Came true,
I long to see you,
Happy.

I saw those feathers,
And,
It reminded me,
That you are,
Forever,
Watching out,
For me,
Leading me,
Down the right path,
Protecting me,
From harm,
Just like,
You always have.

I don't know what to do,
Because,
The reality,
Is creeping in,
That I won't,
Ever,
See you again.

I look,
At the new year,
All I see,
Is a year,
Without you.

I scroll past,
The notes in my phone,
It's almost like,
A diary,
Of those last months,
Of your life,
I can't bare,
To look,
To remember,
I can only,
Hope,
You're floating,
In a better,
Happier,
Place.

I'd have hoped,
That I felt,
Somewhat,
Normal now,
But truthfully,
I don't really,
Know,
What's normal,
Now.

I dreamt,
That you,
Came back to me,
Last night,
It was almost,
Like all the,
Things I've wished for,
Came true,
But I woke up,
And realised,
Not all dreams,
Can come true.

They say grief,
Has 5 stages,
But there are,
So many,
I couldn't even count.

In everything,
I do,
I can't help,
But think,
You should be there,
You should be here.

Hold them close,
Hold them dear,
I promise,
They are always,
Here,
They are always,
Near.

I did my,
Usual routine,
Sitting in my,
Usual coffee shop,
Notebook and pen,
In hand,
It was a glimpse,
At how my life,
Once was,
And how,
My life will,
Never be,
Again.

What surprised me,
More than anything,
Was in all that,
I thought I had lost,
I'd actually lost so,
Much more,
I'd lost friendships,
Family,
Relationships deteriorated,
Quicker than those,
Last breaths you took,
And it's just when,
You think that,
Things can't change,
Any more than they already have,
They do,
Just like that.

Don't hate me,
For carrying on,
You're still,
In every part,
Of my soul.

What am I,

Without you.

You may find yourself,
Doing strange things,
Thinking things,
You may never have,
Thought before,
But remember,
There is no way,
To mourn correctly.

I looked up,
What grief actually means,
We surround the word,
With loss,
But it actually means,
To suffer mentally,
So I question,
Why do we use this word,
Because when you,
Lose someone,
You suffer,
Mentally,
Physically,
Emotionally,
Unconditionally.

Would you believe me,
When I say,
You changed everything,
What was life,
Without you,
What is life,
Without you.

What better way to explain,
How loss makes you feel,
Than having a party,
With no life of it.

I was weak,
But so were you,
I had to leave,
I couldn't rely,
On you.

Life faded out,
Just like that.
A few moments,
It was over.
Just like that.

There's something,
So loud,
And so,
Deafening,
When you,
Hear that,
A loved one,
Has gone,
Imagine,
You are screaming,
But,
There is no noise.

I wonder if people can see,
All the grief plastered,
All over me,
But I remember,
People only see,
What they want to see.

My heart drowned,
The day,
I saw you dwindle,
It kept trying to,
Come up for air,
It wanted to sink,
But it wouldn't dare,
It just kept,
Going,
Until the day,
You left,
And all it could do,
Was tear.

Broken?
More like,
Dismembered.

I constantly,
Try to remember,
That there cannot be,
Joy,
Without sorrow,
But,
They both seem,
To swallow me.

Months down the line,
They say it gets better,
But the reality is,
That each day is.
One further from the last time,
You saw them,
Spoke to them,
Felt them.

After someone is gone,
Everyone rushes in,
They show up,
They show you,
They are there,
Then slowly,
Life goes back to,
Their normal,
Whilst you are left,
In your new normal,
Wondering how,
Lonely this new normal,
Will be.

Maybe,
We should all talk more,
Freely about death,
Because,
Maybe that will be,
What we need,
To live more freely,
To make life,
That little bit more easy.

If you were to close your eyes,
And scribble with a pen,
On this,
Very page,
That is what grief is like.

# Beholden

*Adjective [after verb]*

*Owing thanks or having a duty to someone in return for help or a service.*

It doesn't matter,
Because,
Your time is not over,
The higher power,
Is not ready for you.

The quiet,
Can bring peace,
Serenity,
Sincerely,
I'll surrender,
In harmony.

New horizons,
New blessings,
New beginnings,
New lessons.

Make space in your heart,
For new love to blossom,
You don't have to,
Throw away the loves from before,
Keep them,
They'll remind you,
How love looked then,
And how,
It looks now.

It isn't wrong,
If your heart is truly in the right place.

- *Pure intentions are what matters.*

Normalise showing your love for people,
That you think of them,
That you value them,
That you love them.

Practice patience,
Healing,
Takes time.

Remember your legacy,
Is more than what,
You have achieved,
More than the money,
You have earned,
More than the things,
You have bought,
Your legacy is,
How you treat others,
How you,
Treat the world,
Your legacy,
Is you.

Forever,
I'll be indebted,
To those,
Who held me up,
When I was,
Ready to,
Fall down.

Surround yourself with friends,
Not fans.

I love,
Love,
To see it,
Feel it,
Be in it,
Embody it,
Rationalise it,
Overthink it,
Miss it,
Want it,
To love it,
I love,
Love.

That's when I knew,
That this,
Was something different,
I found my words,
After so long,
With so little to say.

After losing,
I could never,
Bring myself,
To stay,
Where I wasn't,
Truly,
Wanted,
Truly,
Loved.

Happy Mother's Day,
And I am,
So happy to say,
That to all the,
Mother's in my life,
But,
My mother is missing,
From my life,
It doesn't mean to say,
That I don't wish,
Every mother,
The best fucking day,
But allow me,
Because as much,
As there is light,
There is loss,
There is a daughter,
Without a mother,
And so mother,
I pay homage to you,
To your strength,
Love,
Fight,
My life,
Is dedicated to,
Living,
Exactly how you would,
Have liked me to,
Mama,
I love you,
And,
Mamas,
I love you too.

It's hard to see,
The silver lining,
When you want to,
Lie in,
Bed all day,
But I promise,
That lining,
Will be shining,
One day..

Years later,
I still write,
About love,
It just goes to show,
That,
Real love,
Never dies.

Paradise is amazing,
The only thing,
That could make it better,
Would be you.

I stay humble,
In this love,
This life,
I give it everything,
Just so,
I know,
That you know,
I gave it,
Everything I am.

I look at life,
All I've seen,
Been through,
And,
As much as I have,
Prayed,
Wished,
Hoped,
That things were different,
That I could change,
Everything,
Without everything,
I would be nothing.

It's not that I don't,
Care,
Or that I no long,
Hold love for you,
My mental space,
Just can't,
Keep baring,
The weight,
Of your issues,
I love you,
And I'm here,
But for now,
I just need to be,
Here,
For me.

There was something,
About writing this,
Book,
That made me focus,
So deeply,
On creating,
Something,
To share,
With the world,
Something,
That will be,
Timeless.

With every breath,
You are with me,
With every minute,
You are watching,
Out for me.

It's not often you meet,
Someone who loves the,
Same thing you do,
Sour,
Sweet,
And everything in between.
You can be the lemon,
And I'll be the salt.

-    *Salty Lemons Pt 2*

Despite all that I have lost,
All,
Is not lost.

If I ever wrote a poem about you,
I hope that humbles,
You enough to know,
That once upon a time,
You touched my soul,
Enough,
To make me pick up a pen,
And engrave those,
Feelings into paper,
A poem,
That will last forever.

Please don't allow,
Anything by to make you turn into a shell,
Of yourself,
You are not empty,
There's so much you can do,
So much,
You will do.

Forever,
I will continue to do,
My little rituals.
They keep me alive,
Go for coffee,
Write,
Those are the things,
I need to survive.

Your intentions,
Are truly your own,
Everyone else,
Can only,
Speculate.

I cannot say this,
Loud enough,
I did not ask,
For this position,
It was,
Asked of me,
And I played it,
Wholeheartedly.

Look around,
Open your eyes,
And see,
Who has the ability,
To save you,
From yourself.

If you ever,
Played a part in,
Fixing me,
Then you helped,
Make me,
And if you helped make me,
Then please,
Don't hesitate,
To thank yourself,
For all,
That you are.

You can always tell,
When someone has lost,
In the same way,
As you,
There is a bond,
That grief brings,
So in all that you've lost,
You have to remember,
You have also gained.

Whatever you think,
Is truly what's best,
The consequences,
People's actions,
Are not in your control.

I don't count the days you have been gone,
You live timelessly,
In my soul.

- *It's as if I only saw you yesterday.*

Death will either draw you to people,
Or pull you apart,
And in all that has gone,
I still have my brother and sisters,
Our bond is still strong.

# <u>Divine</u>

*adjective (GOD-LIKE)*

*Connected with a god, or like a god.*

My love is unconditional,

And unconditional love,

Is not something I need from you,

I love you,

Just to love you,

Because I love,

All that we have been through,

I love that we have had,

Ups and downs,

Been through the most,

But most of all,

I love that you are,

My place of safety,

That I don't have to question,

If you would be there for me,

I would be dumb to force myself,

To stop feeling,

Stop believing,

In you,

In how I love you,

It doesn't even matter,

If you love me too,

Because I love me,

I love you,

And,

I love us.

Have you ever felt so free,
Where you no longer,
Feel obliged to keep,
Playing nice,
Where you can say,
You don't give a fuck,
And truly mean it.

In acceptance,

There is peace.

I'm fighting for my peace,
And you can't stop me,
All I want is to feel free,
Be in bliss,
Be with me,
I found my voice,
Now I will speak,
I've found my self love,
And now I deserve to be,
At one with me,
Nobody,
Can tell me I am wrong,
That I have to put up with shit,
That I have to continue to be strong,
If you're not adding to my peace
Then I can't keep giving,
Pieces of my soul.

In the end,
The only thing,
That matters,
Is how,
You feel,
About you.

I'm not your clown,
This is not,
Your circus.

Tattooed him,
On my,
Heart,
Soul,
Body,
Hoping,
One day,
He would grace it,
With those,
Beautiful lips.


And one day,
He did.

In the end,
Your strength,
Will always,
Shine through.

I've longed to be loved,
The way,
I love,
But that door,
Was always just,
Slightly ajar,
But here I am,
Arms wide open,
Love,
I'm inviting you in.

I hope,
That in every,
Single,
Moment,
You know,
Just how much,
You matter.

Living so freely,
In my recklessness,
Maybe,
I'll wreck less.

Empty pages,
Empty phases,
Empty promises,
Empty people,
Eventually,
All that,
Will,
Be,
Fulfilled.

Bring me blessings,
I've had enough,
Lessons.

If you deny love,
You're denying,
The core,
Of,
You,
Your world,
Your life.

I love it but I hate it,
Putting my heart on the line,
Another time,
All this risk,
Where's the chocolate biscuit?

I see you,
Keep searching,
For me,
Men like you,
Never forget,
A woman,
Like me.

Let the bliss,
Take over,
Enjoy it,
Live in the present,
Simply,
Be present.

Got me wondering,
Who sent you,
This shit,
Is too good,
Be true.

Each day is,
One step closer,
Sometimes,
The actions,
Are worth the consequences.

The bookshelves are always so,
Full of poetry about love,
And I love,
That we all,
Love,
Love so much.

# __Melancholy__

*Adjective*

*Sadness that lasts for a long period of time, often without any obvious reason.*

I tried,
And that is all one person can do,
Went against my ego's wishes,
And went on different,
But it made no difference to you,
I just wanted to show you,
How I care for you,
That I value you,
More than my own mindset,
I changed my mindset,
So I could reassure you,
I don't understand,
What more I could do,
So when you come,
And act like,
I was the one who gave up on you,
I refuse to apologise,
Say sorry,
I'm not sorry,
That I tried.

And sometimes,
They're not the one who is hurting,
Your feelings,
Sometimes,
You're hurting your own.

Don't ignore your gut.

Sometimes people,
Are simply not meant for you,
It doesn't matter,
How much you hold on,
They will never be for you,
They don't belong with you,
They never did.

It will fall,
How it is going,
To fall.

I walked away,
Silently,
In the hopes,
That you would,
Hear,
The silence,
So loud.

When people show me all the reasons,
I shouldn't keep them,
I don't know why,
I always want them to be kept,
Maybe that's what keeps me,
Awake at night,
That you just up and left.

You can't fight,
For someone,
Who never,
Wanted you to.

No matter how good,
It feels,
It's pointless,
If those feelings,
Aren't real.

So far away,
It would only,
Make sense,
That I no longer,
Feel,
Like I want,
To conversate,
With you,
Physical distance,
Means a little bit of,
Mental distance.
Out of sight,
Out of mind.

Forever confused,
That will forever,
Be you.

I can't help but wonder,
If we were,
In a different,
Place,
Time,
Universe,
Space,
Would us be,
Everything that we,
Have been searching for.

Often I wake up,
And wonder,
Why,
Am I awake,
Is it not okay,
If I sleep,
For a thousand,
Years,
But no amount of,
Sleep could,
Ever release me,
I am tired,
Of being,
So fucking,
Tired.

We fear,
What we don't know,
But,
We fear more,
In all that we know.

In my mind,
I leave,
Every day,
In my reality,
I could never.

Isn't that how the story goes,
Right person,
Wrong time.

Eventually,
You have to accept,
That some voids,
Can never even,
Come close,
To being filled.

I see how,
Those,
Ghosts of my past,
Haunt me,
They creep in,
Just when,
Everything,
Is going good,
They are like,
A reminder,
Of everything,
I shouldn't be.

I hear,
Blocking me,
Brings you peace,
Just as much as,
Loving me once did,
Once does.

I pushed,
You pulled,
Until whatever,
We were fighting for,
Was no more.

Each season,
Brings its own challenges,
Sometimes,
There are multiple seasons,
In a day,
And that is normal,
It's okay.

The weight of the world,
Doesn't need to be on,
Your shoulders,
You're not alone.
It's not your fault.
You can't control everything.

It's about,
Finding the balance,
Between who you were,
And,
Who you are.

Where did it all go wrong,
I ask that question,
To you,
Every time,
I get the chance,
Hoping your answer,
Will bring me closure,
But it never does.

You can say sorry,
But what will a sorry do,
If your actions,
Don't follow through.

I looked for guidance,
But there was no one,
To be found,
That's when I learnt,
Some journeys,
Have to be taken,
All on your own.

Some things never change,
When your sleepless nights,
Creep in,
Don't you,
Remember all those nights.


-    *1:42am: Are you awake?*

I have come so far,
But I find,
Myself still in the very same place,
I was before,
How can that be,
That you can feel ,
Like you have made strides,
But at the same time,
You feel you have taken no steps,
At all.

You know it will,
Never be over,
When you would,
Give everything,
Just to have it back.

# <u>Escapism</u>

*noun [ U ]*

*A way of avoiding an unpleasant or boring life, especially by thinking, reading, etc. about more exciting but impossible activities.*

I like to give credit,
Where credit is due,
And I'd like to,
Say thank you,
To each,
Solid,

Inch of you.

Legs spread wide,
Heart,
Follows suit.

It's not supposed,
To be wholesome,
You and I,
Is supposed to be,
As questionable,
As the devil,
That is on both,
Our shoulders,
Yet,
It feels like the most,
Wholesome thing,
We have ever known.

On sight,
Your,
Spirit rises,
For me,
Because,
Of me.

I wondered,
How good life could be,
Then I looked,
At how good you looked,
When you are,
Inside me.

Yes,
The physical,
Is so beautiful,
But the,
Innermost,
Parts of yourself,
Are what I love,
The most.

Block me out,
If that's how,
You get through,
The day,
Just know that,
Thoughts of me,
Will always,
Lead you astray.

And it's when,
I am with you,
Everything else,
Melts away.

I know,
What I deserve,
But,
The toxic,
Is always there,
Temping me.

Let me just express,
Call this a warning,
When,
Two become one,
It's over for you,
Done.

It wasn't until,
I saw the,
Green eyes,
In the sunlight.

-     *The real meaning of golden hour.*

And,

When,

You,

Hit,

That,

Sweet,

Spot,

It,

Drips,

Like,

Your,

Hand,

In,

A,

Honey,

Pot.

The things,
I would do,
To simply,
Be laid out,
In the sun,
With you.

Make what you feel,
Clear to me,
Make it,
Enter,
My soul,
As you,
Physically do.

Touch my,
Soul,
Just so,
I can,
Feel,
Whole,
Again.

You hide from it,
When the truth is,
You would die for it,
End your life,
Just to spend,
One more night with it,
Can't you,
Comprehend,
That your soul is tied,
To mine,
And it takes,
Something short of,
A miracle,
To break it,
Some things,
Aren't supposed to be,
Over,
You are supposed to,
Go through the motions
Swim across oceans,
Contemplate,
It again and again…

...This shit is permanent,
Like a paper to pen,
It's written,
In the skies,
In the stars,
And it will take,
Light years to,
Dim our light,
Our connection,
Shines bright,
Like your eyes,
When they lock with mine,
Baby,
Daddy,
Take time,
You know,
You are mine.

You spark the fire inside.

You said it was love,
It wasn't,
You said it was trust,
But we couldn't,
Jhene told me,
Not to take you on a boat,
For your birthday,
Not to fuck you on a boat,
For your birthday,
Now we're here,
Here in what should,
Have been love,
But yet it was lust,
And now I'm lost,
Wondering,
What direction I go,
In,
Because,
At night,
My mind takes me to you,
Inhales you,
I can't cum,
Without you...

… So what do I do,
When I remember,
Those lips,
The way we kiss,
The way we stare,
Into each other's souls,
Then I suck your soul,
Then you lick,
Away my problems,
Your tongue knows,
How to solve them,
We both reach new heights,
We fuck,
In the lights,
So we can see,
Not just feel,
We know,
This is real.

So wrong,
But it's so right,
I want you,
On top,
On,
Sight.

The words come,
As quickly,
As the urge you have,
To taste me,
Something about it,
So beautiful,
So toxic,
So needy.

# **Preservation**

*noun [ U ]*

*The act of keeping something the same or of preventing it from being damaged.*

I swear,
Poems haven't really,
Come into my mind,
Until you came around,
You have to be my muse,
Because I wouldn't,
Even be writing this,
If it wasn't for you,
You don't know,
How long I have waited,
To feel something,
Other than all the things,
I am going through,
I go through it,
But I can't explain it,
To anyone,
You understand,
And I don't have to explain,
Because you know,
You understand pain,
You make it easier,
To feel less ashamed,
You make me feel safe.

Tell me what you need to feel safe.

Your emotional self,
Is not you,
It's a part of you,
And so,
Don't react in the moment,
Take some time,
Focus.

In those darkest storms,
Let me be your light,
In your cold nights,
Let my shoulder be the one you lean on,
When you're trapped,
Let me be your escape,
When you're scared,
Let me be your safe place.

Have they seen all of you?
All those parts of you,
That you push,
A little to the side,
In the hopes,
That they don't recognise,
The trauma that,
Lives inside you,
What would they do,
If you exposed,
Those things,
You choose to ignore,
Imagine,
A time,
A place,
A day,
A person,
Where you can,
Just be you.

See how I know,
You were meant for me,
Because you,
Look at me like,
No time has passed,
Like the building of,
You and I,
Isn't full of stained glass,
See I know that,
What you feel is real,
Because you feel it,
And all you feel is real,
Like you're safe,
Like you're at home,
Maybe,
This is the only home,
You have known,
Maybe you,
Feel so unsafe,
In the safety of this home,
Because trouble is,
All that you've known,
Relax,
Take your time,
With me,
You're safe,
At home.

Give me space,
Give me freedom,
Give me peace,
Take me,
To my chosen place.

It's those small,
Acts,
Of kindness,
Of love,
That,
Are the things,
That tie my.
Soul to yours.

You shouldn't have to,
Sell yourself to them,
You are not an item,
For the highest bidder,
To claim,
You are priceless,
Everything you are,
Is you,
So don't be ashamed.

One day,
I hope you,
See,
How peaceful,
Life could be.

Don't just let me in,
Let me inside,
There's only so long,
You can hide,
I'm here now,
Here for the ride.

What better,
Feeling,
Than feeling,
Like you are safe.

Think about where,
In the world,
You truly feel,
Safe,
Go there,
Make home there.

Instinctively,
I always go into,
Protection mode,
Protecting me,
Protecting you.

There's a place,
In which you,
Can be at peace,
With everything,
You have been through,
With all the people,
Who have been there,
Or went astray,
Where your peace,
Takes pride of place,
I hope to see you,
There soon.

Someone once asked me,
If I had ever been in love,
The kind of love,
Where you can't see your,
Life without them,
Settle with them,
And my issue with,
That kind of love,
Is that it it's all based on,
Conditions,
If we are together,
What the future plans are,
If we are,
Settled,
Unsettled,
If you are no longer here,
Or if I am not,
For me,
My love,
Is unconditional.

I am,
My own,
Safety net,
But that net needs,
A strong foundation,
I have,
Saved myself,
So many times,
Only with the,
Help of my,
Day ones,
Hands.

I am open to,
The love I give,
I give it,
With nothing expected,
In return,
It brings me serenity,
To be loving,
To keep loving.

When you watch the world go by,
What goes through your mind,
I always wonder,
What people are dealing with,
Wonder if their life is as,
Chaotic as mine is,
There is some calm,
In knowing,
That you probably aren't alone,
In chaos.

When they left me,
I looked for,
Poems I could relate to,
Because I couldn't write,
So I hope,
That these poems,
This writing,
Makes you feel better,
Less alone.

If you keep watering a plant,
It simply keeps living,
Breathing,
So think about what would happen,
If you stopped,
Let's apply that,
To us,
Let's give ourselves,
Love.

I hope that whatever,
You are facing,
You still find joy,
In the little things.

Being content is all I Long for,
Just feeling like,
I don't need to take deep breaths,
To control the anxiety,
Breathe to live,
Not to exist.

When you put yourself,
Under so much pressure,
Does it make you feel better,
Or does it distract you,
From all that you are going through,
What if you,
Could be free,
Free to feel.

How do you still practice,
Self love,
Without feeling selfish,
You have to believe,
You still deserve to love,
Though it may not,
Be deemed appropriate,
But fuck whats appropriate,
You can still love you,
Despite what others think,
Despite how they feel about you.

Life is so chaotic,
But what the trick is,
It's to find those moments of calm,
Stillness,
And hone into them,
The chaos still continues,
But you can be,
A spectator for once.

In the midst of chaos,
Remember who you are.


-   *From Coffee, a Notebook and Self Love.*

The following page contains a letter that I wrote weeks before my mum was admitted to the hospital.

We were told that she was going to pass away, it was only a matter of time.

And so, one day I was alone with her in the hospital where she was pretty much unresponsive and read it to her.

I do not know if she heard me, but I believe she did.

Shortly after she had a rush of energy which lasted weeks and within those weeks she told me that we should be telling each other that we love each other more.

On the day she passed away, the nurse present told me that the last words I said were the last ones she probably ever heard.

*'We all love you so much mum, you have been so strong and we are so proud of you'*

Dear mum,

I'm sitting here, at your bedside watching you in some kind of sleep. I know the end is coming, that in a short time I'll no longer be able to see your chest move as you take a breath, that I won't be able to see your face with my own eyes. I'm sorry that you have had to suffer through this process, that was the last thing I ever wanted. I didn't think things would end this way for you. I can't take in everything that's happening, I feel like I'm running on autopilot. You are such a fighter, you beat odds that were never ever in your favour. Even though you may not have beat your illness, you defo tried to kick the shit out of it.

I can only thank you, not for just being my mum but for allowing me to take care of you in one of the hardest times of your life. You trusted me, believed in me and you knew that I always had your back. It has been the biggest achievement of my life, that I could be there for you, make you feel safe and that I could give you some of the care you gave me.

People who have never even met you will feel a type of loss because there is simply nobody like you. I hope that I do you proud, that your spirit continues to live through your children and grandchildren. We are your legacy.

I promise you that I will do all the things you wanted me to, that I will fulfil your wishes and that I will live the way you wanted me to. What would I be without your unconditional love, banter and caring nature. You gave us so much, the sacrifices you made, the lessons mean more than you will have ever known. You shaped me, I am here and who I am because of you.

Our relationship has been that of a typical mother and daughter but I'm glad that you left this world being more than my mum, you became one my best friends, especially in these last few years.

Dalj, you're one of a fucking kind, thank you for blessing my life with your presence.

You may leave, but you will never be gone.

I love you, unconditionally.


Sonam.

Printed in Great Britain
by Amazon

82130902R00123